...ING
...O SHOW THA...
...OES NOT DISAPPE...
...S WHEN I DISAPPEAR
...NOT DISAPPEAR
...SHOULD ACHIEVE THIS
...L I FEEL MORE OR LESS ISOL...
THE CONTINUING PROGRESSION
A PARALYSIS I CAN ONLY PATHOLOGIZE
NOT A MASK &
TIME OVER WHICH IT CLOSES, THAT
SOME CHOPPED-UP TENSION B/W
...ITUDE & COLLECTIVITY, NOT THAT
...DISAPPEARS INTO
...OWN VOICE BELOW
...CONFRONTATION WITH ANONYM...
...MIGHT'VE IMAGINED HERE.
...TER DELIRIUM THAN DRIFT I...
REPRESENTATIONS.
...TTER ANTICIPATE A
...NGEALED POSTURE
...ELSE BE EFFACED AS
THE OBJECT
...OF K...

I Want Something Other Than Time

I Want Something Other Than Time
Copyright © Lewis Freedman, 2021

ISBN 978-1-946433-78-7
First Edition, First Printing, 2021

Ugly Duckling Presse
The Old American Can Factory
232 Third Street #E-303
Brooklyn, NY 11215
uglyducklingpresse.org

Distributed in the USA by SPD/Small Press Distribution
Distributed in the UK by Inpress Books

Cover design by Sarah Lawson
Typesetting by dourmoose
The type is Bembo

Printed and bound at McNaughton & Gunn
Covers printed letterpress at Ugly Duckling Presse

The publication of this book was made possible by a grant from the New York State Council on the Arts with the support of Governor Andrew Cuomo and the New York State Legislature, along with support from the National Endowment for the Arts and the Robert Rauschenberg Foundation.

I Want Something Other Than Time

Lewis Freedman

Ugly Duckling Presse, 2021

Contents

I Want Something Other than Time   1

I Want Something Other than Time   2

I Want Something Other than Time   3

I Want Something Other than Time   4

I Want Something Other than Time   5

I Want Something Other than Time   6

I Want Something Other than Time   7

I Want Something Other than Time   8

I Want Something Other than Time   9

I Want Something Other than Time   10

I Want Something Other than Time   11

I Want Something Other than Time   12

I Want Something Other than Time   13

I Want Something Other than Time   14

I Want Something Other than Time   15

I Want Something Other than Time   16

I Want Something Other than Time	17
I Want Something Other than Time	18
I Want Something Other than Time	19
I Want Something Other than Time	20
I Want Something Other than Time	21
I Want Something Other than Time	22
I Want Something Other than Time	23
I Want Something Other than Time	24
I Want Something Other than Time	25
I Want Something Other than Time	26
I Want Something Other than Time	27
I Want Something Other than Time	28
I Want Something Other than Time	29
I Want Something Other than Time	30
I Want Something Other than Time	31
I Want Something Other than Time	32
I Want Something Other than Time	33
I Want Something Other than Time	34

I Want Something Other than Time	35
I Want Something Other than Time	36
I Want Something Other than Time	37
I Want Something Other than Time	38
I Want Something Other than Time	39
I Want Something Other than Time	40
I Want Something Other than Time	41
I Want Something Other than Time	42
I Want Something Other than Time	43
I Want Something Other than Time	44
I Want Something Other than Time	45
I Want Something Other than Time	46
I Want Something Other than Time	47
I Want Something Other than Time	48
I Want Something Other than Time	49
I Want Something Other than Time	50
I Want Something Other than Time	51
I Want Something Other than Time	52

I Want Something Other than Time	53
I Want Something Other than Time	54
I Want Something Other than Time	55
I Want Something Other than Time	56
I Want Something Other than Time	57
I Want Something Other than Time	58
I Want Something Other than Time	59
I Want Something Other than Time	60
I Want Something Other than Time	61
I Want Something Other than Time	62
I Want Something Other than Time	63
I Want Something Other than Time	64
Acknowledgments	66

The hope for a better society and the despair of solitude, both of which are founded on experiences that claim to be self-evident, seem to be in an insurmountable antagonism.

— Emmanuel Levinas

If I'm not me, who is me? And when I'm myself, what am I? And if this isn't presence, when is it?

— Mishna Avos

O I shall go as arguing redemption, as the unconsumed are ashamed
In the company of nothing, a prisoner of the balances,
The husks of the field, (confoundation of envy.)
While the forehead of sorrow soulders bladed confusion
With wisdom of people spawning in failure,

— Merle Hoyleman

I Want Something Other Than Time

The aim of this writing
is to show that
I does not disappear.
Even when I disappear I
does not disappear.
If I should achieve this
will I feel more or less isolated
in the continuing progression
of a paralysis I can only pathologize?
It's not a mask &
the time over which it closes, that's not it,
not some chopped-up tension b/w
solitude & collectivity, not that.
I disappears into my own voice below
the confrontation with anonymity we
might've imagined here.
Better delirium than drift in
my representations.
Better anticipate
a congealed posture or
else be effaced as
the object
of knowledge.

I Want Something Other Than Time

My way of proceeding
in which I no longer hear
the voice aside from its echo
might've become banal
even to me.
Like my incommunicable remains
form a barricade against unity
but this time it's not news to me anymore.
My tie bares a picture of death for the whole
office to see but it can't even be called
death b/c its significance has been abolished
(it's a tie).
It's a window that, having withdrawn entirely
from the outside it had asserted itself for
centuries to separate, now conceives of any
situation as an enlargement of "every place
is in another place."
My foundation has become my modesty
offended by my living mouth.
There's nothing clear to the dare
I feel in Nietzsche's words,
"I am dead b/c I am stupid."
Horrible.
But now at least
the page
feels full.

I Want Something Other Than Time

Some thing that is
no longer hears
all that is told.
Instead, a last convulsion is
at work joining
beginningless fragments at
evanescent extremes.
Either it's something which arrives from itself
or it's an inversion of that new spacing where
we receive nothing from the past.
The past, R I P, an obligation which will
never take place, to restore a self-constitution,
to restore the not-to-be, its revealed traits,
to uselessness.
There is a leak in my consciousness
so that the function of the present,
to preside like some mantra over self-relation,
only budges in the new spacing.
Signs no longer
experiencing the surface.

I Want Something Other Than Time

There is this
meaningless elation,
moment of total joy, to
arrive in the bad times when
preference no longer feels actionable.
We doused our hair in listerine &
sang our new song as though coaxed by
the formal structure of jubilation.
There was no room for distance, there was
only the contrary, only the contrary contrary.
This sentence you see is veiled in decency.
It is, as though by limiting itself
to a kid's game, as though it were interchangeable.
But it's really a game as fixed as
the rich slumming it to feel how their power
exists everywhere.
Each time we are accosted by paralysis
we close again our approach to the
future while the future
in its privilege
remains open.

I Want Something Other Than Time

I wish us to be
in some exceptional
place, but my heart is
so full of it, so all contact
is mystery & we must
begin so often in struggle it's
fused to an end.
All dimensions become impossible.
All communications accomplish
only self-construction.
All selves fixed in a withdrawn being borne,
the space b/w us free w/o reason.
I want a contact that's more than
some notion of not-knowing,
an initiation that's more
than what some child-god of myself
feels obliged to admit.

I Want Something Other Than Time

I remember
writing this thirteen
years ago leaning
against the wall &
it was willing then to say "there
is nothing most private in me" so
why can't it now?
The nothing of a secrecy proffered &
abdicated at so little cost we have
no idea but in perhaps I don't or do exist.
Tempted to commit ourselves against
anticipation to resuscitate the sentence but
somehow move towards no longer transmitting it.
If the content is incommunicable, I said,
then pronounce nothing.
"Shut Fuck," you said,
you were already foundational here,
"already existing
isn't something to wait for."

I Want Something Other Than Time

When the fabric ignores,
you know the fabric
I'm dramatizing here,
that possibility is irremissibly
the bridge of itself,
leaving us full
of a domestic reasoning, an
enchainment, a mittance riveted
to the world we live,
in a paralyzed mirror of
contingency regarding itself.
It's not like I've studied it.
It's like I'm like my stupid double,
but more abandoned,
& next to me is a silver
tomb I'm riveted to
some nascent kernel of
wishful joy
in the muddying
shine of
its reflection.

I Want Something Other Than Time

This doesn't
express our need for
deliverance with either
the light or grace I'm
waiting for.
It simply exposes itself as though
the need to have written were the
new truth in a trance.
As though desire for something other
than time could ever be the absence,
read that again …
could ever be eleven eleven (the number
inside the figure eight).
But hasn't less time passed in this
manifest than we pretended to think?
Aren't we more & less forgetful,
more & less alone than we are?
Take it away,
& encumbered by the
heave the band
plays the passage
again.

I Want Something Other Than Time

I announce something
so I can call that
something unreal. So
having unhappened, I can be like,
how could you call it that?
You see it's my dream to say
there can be a thing not attached as itself.
Pivot. Signal. Pivot.
I'm fucking up again b/c the inflection
of my mastery is off.
If free of our dreams, we could be the first
folk to never take place, which
of all our fucked-up supernumerary
dreams is the one
I dream again of forgetting.
Later I'll appear to face some
trace of the blocked epiphany with
a shrug saying,
the something has power b/c
it makes the grip it
gets legal, & the sign
of its pivoting
gavel won't let go.

I Want Something Other Than Time

I'll try & say
this again like I'm
saying it to my mum.
When the weather is consummate
with our moods we go outside just
like that. We take a walk, which is to
say we are thinking in sentences, &,
as though it were a perfect accident to be ourselves,
we calculate each sentence from the center & back.
However, there's something else we're not thinking of,
a calculation in the ratio of visible sky
to steps that the sentence incurs by
overextending it so that what we are
lacking is what we're looking at &
we can't look further into that.
Then if we were to step away, to try
& absorb, for example, the whole page
as one instant,
we'd find a wait in
the arc that
exceeds the
end.

I Want Something Other Than Time

A bank-teller
slapped a bank-teller.
That's all I've got left.
The limits of which we shall
soon see.
A bank-teller slapped a bank-teller.
Without irony I've been there,
have recognized & discovered myself there.
A frozen pizza.
We can receive nothing from ourself but the past.
The charges were dropped.
Soon every possible word will have been
& will be a pun.
It feels pure to exude w/o irony
a power of total renewal,
but the sentence given
will still require a verb
& go cartoonish,
a remainder of precisely
this
produced as
that.

I Want Something Other Than Time

I wanted to have
already read it,
to have already written it,
to have already heard the alarm
& reached the end.
Some hero blows back this sign before
it becomes what becomes true.
The heavens with no eye on earth.
We want that supreme irresponsibility.
I just want us to know how obstinately I
stick to my suffering,
as if some faint sign has emerged in the margins
to cut short across the void again of self-knowledge
& it inscribes my name.
Backed up against the subject again
& we are designating us the heroes.
At least the instant will have gone
back there.
Shake shake, sleep sleep.
Fifty years later,
it's me again.

I Want Something Other Than Time

A luminous
nourishment, we
get bogged down eating
light, mobilizing what's
already thrown back its momentum
like a bathroom light switch
materialized only by the inertia of habit.
Not caring for weight in this hole of chatter,
truth is like the least memorable,
the least mobile thing.
I don't wanna move my two books b/c
thing becomes thought & thought thinks its
only success would be to become thing.
Can I escape truth's gravity into this
hole of chatter?
My dad was there, my dad was there
in this fake
final accounting
of action.

I Want Something Other Than Time

They is a gas, aghast,
unwilling to relinquish
their gourds, unwilling to
relinquish what I see as my special
bond with writing, the cushioned
pursuit of a relationship to everything.
My community, though
profitably absorbed in its jectivity,
never laughs at a joke from beyond our walls.
Even now we're praying for the world's
support, though we've designated us
the discernable humming &
cast them as some prerequisite chasm lotion.
That said, everybody, them & us,
agree the pregnantless heavens can
take away death. And when we feel
a toolbox of light leaping from
our hearts we know it's
a small blood ransom god
letting in
the good
progress of freedom.

I Want Something Other Than Time

Not only my misfortune
to be preoccupied with
salvation, or,
if the world has no substance
then well, you know …
growth will never carry our commission.
Most of my concerns
are frivolous moralities rank with representational
desires, with sad confrontations around my
stolen proficiencies, so let's instead,
accountless as we are,
be diverted by the fragments of our simple
forgetfulness, by the playful designation
of idiot you have waited for nothing,
feeling it optimistically as yes,
there is nothing to overcome.
Strange joy to play
ourselves as
beyond our
claim.

I Want Something Other Than Time

Either something is
happening that we can't
grasp or my anxious dyspepsia
is writing this for me.
An ensuing shape, it will
be completed, oblivious to everything,
but it's not eloquent.
Perhaps there's no sequel to a narrative of our first
continuous becoming, & the death of the individual subject
as economic driver will summate common era history
"from which no rebirth may be effected."
My retinue doesn't buy it.
But in the same breath we are bound to admit
a meaning drawn from contradiction is facile,
& maybe there's no difference b/w spring &
cigarette, b/w time & a fiction of itself,
b/w Bartleby & the 1% (interlaced
with the guts we
refuse to
understand).

I Want Something Other Than Time

This is why I
wrote that nothing can
happen if it's read.
But no worries,
nothing can ever be decently
clothed enough to be read.
Not even this exigent breathing now
as a form to life or as time passing
can be satisfactorily reabsorbed
into its illusory having happened.
My foot
as if it weren't suspended to walk condemned
within a what we can say as if we can say it.
Sometimes I'm wondering if there is no place,
only language as a circulating account
for the circumstances of power.
Sometimes I'm wondering if
there's only place,
this flat
denial.

I Want Something Other Than Time

Is it knowledge
or is it magic that
encompasses everything in
my life?
My ego looks to the light of my ego
& presides,
providing forwards as though my future
identity had already come to me.
The sock, incapable of rational knowledge
once removed from the foot can find no reason.
Does it lie there in total relation to itself
overloading the ground?
Because my encounter is clearly somehow about
loss, about what I must've in the beginning
turned immemorial for this intuition of
what will come next to remain,
b/c of this, b/c the other dimensions of
light around this light will regard
but not surmount it,
I'm too wrapped up to speculate
on the result of this thing,
to care for its render-
ing of me &
poem srsly
who
cares?

I Want Something Other Than Time

What this paper sketches
& what I sketch
are two simultaneous seams
(seems like former sight / ulcered
time), & this is not speaking speaking
or an epigraph to what will follow.
What will follow will be a question of what
happened enslaved to the question of what is
happening again expressed by a consumptive
shadow beginning "let it be understood" or
"I willingly admit."
Not a single fucking thing,
or so often being in that to
remain to ignore.
If we could remove this from itself,
would it be
a deduction
or a preservation
of itself?

I Want Something Other Than Time

In the dream
I am smoking again,
saying again, it has all
been a dream since I quit.
In the mirror
your reflection finally tells me
there is no better self
after all
intention is a description
& contains the limits of description vis-à-vis
what thought won't approach.
I made an itinerary for the day
but I can't stop demanding something incomparable
to weigh in the weight of the code
that will confer
that what doesn't yet exist
recruits me.
Me, perhaps willfully ignorant
of all real things.
Me,
& not my intention.

I Want Something Other Than Time

The aim of this
writing is to be
an example to itself,
a condition for a condition, a
fixed point for our own irreconcilable
part, useful b/c we won't leave it behind.
But how are we going to approach the
spatial orienting of this body existing
when we are in this screen in this room?
It's obvious we don't have to be there when
something happens to us,
but even in the anonymity of
what we've fallen into
there's something about the domain of us,
something like a certain space immobile
but raining.
Something about the fact of several
million years ago
not here
murmur
here.

I Want Something Other Than Time

Our mind's work is
to produce an unconscious
that, in waves, diffuses &
transposes our wishes & fears.
We are "broken b/w two poles of vacuity."
I can't seem to locate, let alone
master an average of my efforts.
When I sit down to try I find
I'm harnessed to some frame that's
not the work at hand.
A capacity to cogently report these
difficulties is delivered as a whole
to myself to bolster a fiction of
something foundational, evoke the
floating wires which network us w/o
room for distance.
But if identity carves thought
to issue identity's
management ...
how can we open others to us
w/o resolving ourselves in
mastery?

I Want Something Other Than Time

We are thrown by our
work to be a stranger
who maintains this stance:
that the weight of feeling, in all
its electric multiples, can be
addressed only thru a strangeness
that, as a matter of stupidity, we have,
enveloping it in mystery, reserved for
ourself as public, possessing, for a moment,
neither one nor the other.
It's as though in my desire to transcend this
I would change my given name to
public, the sound it's said with
now conforming to indicate a
deappropriated relation to my life.
I, synonym for power,
relinquish my merge with
this object in its
creation to
the public
domain.

I Want Something Other Than Time

There is no victory
over death, guys.
The death guys free themselves
making themselves uncategorizable
again & again
the end an elastic dominion,
artifice for us.
I was recruited to be a poet, but our world,
one of indefinite centers, has all the imitation,
gnosis, & intermediaries it could burn (even
this exceptional fatigue). Whatever. There
being no splice to disclose us further,
we still need private languages to bear
eros into touch, to pass ourselves into
attunement, to pass as imminent sonorous
things.
The sun, you say, remains unintelligible.
I'm like, ditto the parent. All
these alchemical codes
inscribing us to
live by thoughts,
to scale
time.

I Want Something Other Than Time

Do not take it
personally.
I don't take it personally.
Lacking the coordinating fiber,
each joint goes ever a not now
to not know what's happening in
the when it happens.
But by turning the poem suddenly towards
an intelligible sun to imitate
a world of light w/o being able to,
I believe I heard it sharpening in the front yard
networked with whatever loss we'd hoped to
skip over in assuming the subject.
I wouldn't do that either, believe me.
Our conditions for my obligation
feel trivial b/c my lean-to
increases as it's skipped. We might
guess the console, you might say, but
it's no consolation,
it's undeniably
attached to
the neck.

I Want Something Other Than Time

I'm hesitant to
begin by climbing up
plastic into the old sky.
I hesitate before writing
today is not a point to investigate
today b/c it's first a return to its
own form, has nothing to do with today.
Instead a confusion about community, about
how to listen to having heard a conversation
of dust circulating b/w us already before we've
begun, about how fucking up &
condemning ourselves for it, we
might then reunite,
about how to untie an identicality we
turned into thought to incite the delusion
that our secrets are not in common,
about how to just be
when the instant feels completed not
like a memory written
thru, but like
a totally expanding
corruption of
the possible.

I Want Something Other Than Time

Or, for example, to
say this again, there is
no desire we could adequately
wait for.
Consequently, we remain unarriving here.
It's all in the crystal eye, or the repeatable
mechanics of the left arm, such that
no foot steps on another foot like it's stepping on
ground, or the appointment we'll miss to make our
absence thinkable.
I traverse the small, spread-out plains town by foot
like some kind of idiot, an old portrait
slipped thru the centuries only to appear
more withdrawn, the time of its making grown
infinitely small.
Because there are no benches here I only rest publicly
in line at the store.
I look up to the screens.
They're shopping a new series, "Unforgivable Inconsistencies."
Its voices float out from & toward my skull
in recursive jags.
The gap goes less & less fluent, but invents a
fermentation to survive it.
Together, we look like the interval's
orbit, a pitcher of almost-
closed eyes. I want to
carry its unrecognizable
gift across the
room.

I Want Something Other Than Time

Does a situation
exist? No, b/c I'd categorize
it amongst those furnishings
whose tracing of an unforeseeable
triples back to say, "nonetheless
something happened,"
& we say we persevere, I mean
disappear.
We'll have to try & explain an exhaustion
other than tiredness to the improvisatory
turn as it passes from speculation into figment.
I hesitated here b/c there is no memory
before the hand as there is no memory
before I has arrived to crush this
trivia by refusing all prior knowledge.
And now it's broken, you said, remembering
a similar feeling,
a stride thru light to
grasp reserves of
vibration still
talking thru
our faux
mastery of
silence.

I Want Something Other Than Time

Light & resuscitate,
ready to contain the loss
of itself, ready to render
the full paralysis of voice in a
pendant. Sensation of such last
ways of seeing
some past mode of illuminated encounter
its own limit & close
to mistrust the mediations.
Though there is no at the bottom,
there is no at the bottom is a delegation
of separateness from this to that,
the unlimitedness of a test around
the suppressions of history to the direct
arbitrary endurance of the operation of
fact. We do not make things
appear or disappear
except by
repeating them.

I Want Something Other Than Time

If this is subservient
to the relative immobility
of syntax, guarantees
that word like light falls here
in one of three places & in
relation to intelligible sun or
glass eye hiding in suddenly starpit from
where a deep vibrancy affects us, then I'll
flush at point of thought until
it snaps & lifts impersonal in the
contagions of our restrained presence.
Gulp.
I think of a father bringing back
toad in the hole like it's never
been done & chatting on death
"from which no light escapes,"
as though it were end's
syncopated fusion
paradox that
precipitates
syntax's
clairvoyance.

I Want Something Other Than Time

I want something
from those years back.
I whisper the text I'm
reading, but still can't follow
the transition b/w one moment
& another.
Even to say "moment"
is to code an older & complex mystery
whose demands & correspondences
can only be improvised.
The rule of "moment"
is "already excavated,"
like am I writing a book or
in a book more? Or
am I in the middle of this
or in the place of its turn?
Welcome to the sum of not everything
it attempts to say,
I can sense sound,
I can sound
sense.

I Want Something Other Than Time

I want to build a
ladder from my mind
to the mind of matter.
In the cadence of digression, we emanate
the company of all time.
Let's begin again by reversing our reach
&, with the inviolable intensity of our
plasma, offer offense to our inheritance.
Our inheritance is that which gives each
thing form to time (insert cash register sound effect here).
We can feel the mind we share emanating
from the vast spread, & I'd especially
like to thank a different thought I
might witness, some thought cut from the not-thought
that could rid us of thought, or at least the
thought of thought.
Interned to the master of its
enemy, it goes, "I'm not even
attempting this," it
goes, "this isn't,
y'know, attuned
to want."

I Want Something Other Than Time

I've just shown the
impossibility of a memory
securing its future, now
what?
The divine is a preference of the
human, the human the divine,
interwoven whatever.
Ugh, don't worry about the ugh of that bad.
To withdraw from an idea is a blossoming,
a blooming swaying curtain constituted by
the dissolution of a memory which acts upon
it as inside breeze.
But is there a way out of the subject to
whom this will happen?
This poem says no, but does it?
Don't the gaps of its movement refer to
movement in a yet to be of elsewhere?
The future is an outline drawn to
outlive its shape, critical of ignition,
critical of touch, of debt, of all
possibles, & of all
points which
dissolve.

I Want Something Other Than Time

It's set dead
against the flow of
my mind, & the distance
it alone inhabits is an edge
relegated to the mystery of
what the edge is or isn't beyond.
We posit contact, constant contact,
abandoned, yes, clustered, yes, contact.
Obstacle, yes, abstraction, yes, hidden,
yes, an entry, yes, a constant contact we posit.
In the company of release our
eminent board of directors capiches,
refunds the group to conduct the query
again:
Is it the it we were speaking of
(a system of spheres is now
felt rotating against the distance)
or else.

I Want Something Other Than Time

Yes itself
to my voice says,
welcome to the precision
of a situation that doesn't
assume it.
The one cup that tells us drink it
& the one cup that tells us we can't.
Go over there, my voice says,
where there is always a room
& over is a voice wanting out of language,
think what'll happen to music
when we're out of time. Yes,
I can respect that.
My ego's a person & says,
the voice calls on me,
but doesn't let it settle in on being able.
It simply avoids the machine that is
my work.
Between the pretense of two opposing
factions, I'm my stranger
to property, stranger
than
property.

I Want Something Other Than Time

I want to feel ok
right here. I want to
say I'm not wasted
in the choppy paint of
thinks itself, & a dreamy
obedience to the music proceeds me.
As I've said before, a dream might not be
built of representation.
So cheap a ransom where the accident
is almost repeated, is an interior plane of
expiring breath, hello & then let go.
I think the devil's in
going back to a withheld meaning &
letting its deferred presence
prescribe a place we'll never get to.
We're assuming then that
this is one of them, uh,
special clovers, abandoned,
like all things here, to the hype
of liberation.
O mortar get me higher,
the loud voice goes,
move away
from the shore.

I Want Something Other Than Time

Excluded by a method
they resorted to in
dynamizing an intersubjective
void that reads b/w us, I hope
to be able to say, yes, like "the prehistory
of prehistory" of which Lispector writes, yes,
I hope to say, it's not possible to face up to
the event of being momentarily not oneself, of welcoming
this thing b/w us into our moment that's touched in
the same way each time by an appropriated analogy which
likens the network of death to our bodies' nervous systems,
& to let that thing rewrite the pattern of time b/w
two instants & oil again a strung structure of vanishing
thru the whole pore.
If we're its parasite then we're thinking about destiny right
now, we think it's been shrinking for a thousand
years.
And I've resorted to a description of this hope here
b/c we're seriously not held by memory, we're
backed up against our purchases,
backed up against a referent to
time's passing I can't
actually wait
for.

I Want Something Other Than Time

I carried myself
far off from myself.
I wasn't the master,
not of my subject in either
instance, & I couldn't contrast them.
But putting the struggle of reason aside
while still remaining in reason's system,
the explanations multiply until prediction
has yet to come about,
& I'm told that it's the voice of myself
embellishing the voice of myself
to snatch effacement as it pronounces nothing.
Will I admit to what's immobile in me
again? That some new arrangement of
pre-existing elements throws itself at this
immobility to lose control of its phrases?
Sure, b/c we hold revolution in an
assumption of valor that,
even in its command against us,
gathers the self
revived in
recombination.

I Want Something Other Than Time

The need to feel
satisfied disturbs the
beliefs I'm entangled within,
a crisis refusing to awaken an
activism within me, a crisis
that puts my vocations to sleep.
All objections subjected to utterance
become negligible, on equal footing with
the occasional mirage of received language
which never ceases to be falling into the
spaciousness of a space that starts
voiding below me.
Remember that time our inheritance
was tested & we declined to speak?
"Our tears are clerks defiling a
tragedy they know nothing of,"
you said so perfectly, & then with the
other hand I am incapable of loosening
the neck, & I can think, "this is the air
I am breathing," performing it
as the only possible
thought right now.

I Want Something Other Than Time

Last night I dreamt
of a perforation in my
intersubjective space where
the problems of wealth &
power were unworked.
Waking, I realized how dead I am to
the immobility of those things. Correction:
due to the immobility of those structures as they
manifest in intersubjective space, I feel
basically already dead.
But I'm always coming back to my senses from
this, exposed w/o locus to have been here
all along.
Waking, my replacement asked me if we had
breathed the air yet in the room we'd
slept in.
The instability of our fiction, I said, is
measured by excess to remain in us.
It sometimes seems to me, I said,
that our drive for self-annihilation
is affirmed
by our feelings
of hope.

I Want Something Other Than Time

Glissant writes
something like "the child
doesn't exist apart from the
spherical protuberance the child rotates
on their rupture," & I can feel
that by accusing myself in this chair in this
throat that I am still that child.
This must be life for it to feel like we're
writing this.
We are anciently internal, I tell myself, &
I tell myself a ghost eats a ghost cake
they tell me.
A vitamin grabs a hand of life
both b/c the alchemy of the body
seems to depend on a system of twos,
& b/c in my meditation for
no system of any kind
I failed to reassemble,
I failed to marry
the identicals.

I Want Something Other Than Time

According to my
nostalgia a repression
of experience is here &
there is nowhere else.
This is repeating &, as Anna
transcribes, "creates the illusion
of time having stopped." Or,
I believe I can behave as if
I've stopped time.
Like either this isn't today or I'm not in it.
In my too-well-nourished body
nothing is achingly starving, exhausting
each friend of their sign.
Outline of experience going lipless in
the text.
Fluid gathering where an older syntax
is defaced by this.
I'm moved by this. I'm upset. I feel
eternally hostile.
I can suddenly imagine content
as an outline to context,
a shore receding
faster than
waves.

I Want Something Other Than Time

Imagine we've
offended each other
& we're both saying sorry,
it's my fault, our good conscience
feeling guilty & kind.
The whole mood would crash if a fly
landed on the page & walked across it.
We're trying to face up to the dream-fact
that we inebriate the raw words to
wring feeling from them & their
high is precarious, can melt in the
presence of any refractory or even
reciprocal interaction.
Who am I addressing here?
I'm anxious b/c I feel I'm failing to
gather us up in a synchronized
representation, & this anxiety
ruptures the intrigue I wish to hold
about where we might be leading us.
My sense is if it's negotiating
intention, it's not irreducible.
And what I want for us
is a moment of
irreducible
meaning,
continuous.

I Want Something Other Than Time

What we can't understand
we can't but make.
A miracle in place like a
spanner set to sit upon the sea.
A mind which,
fleeced of its fillings,
boggles a stammer in the thoughts around
the writing as it's being written.
Hibernating in the moonstone background
of our resplendent decay, is it all
fusion & loss,
ready to splice into concurrence any two,
no, three things, ready to turn the question
towards a battered globe that's been
all along in this very room, & then,
in a mutage, exit this fixed rejoinder
into a continued hush where microbe
& forcefield are becoming one, no,
three?
The refurbished arms are then
resealed before the
as-new packaging
is fired
shut.

I Want Something Other Than Time

I begin with a
preliminary remark,
a tell-all kind of remark:
to be a patient is to be
free of time.
But to be a patient is to be low-spirited,
is to find that the inversion of suffering
experienced in crying is inverted again thru
repetition. Is it possible to usefully abandon
hope? At least
if we keep on hoping
we'll die with a harness on?
I lift a question, a different question, & I
store it for later (I haven't asked this question
yet). I'm feeling a little pushy, a little
pissed-off in these corroded shadows.
I'm like, "the future is blue," as though
that were a meaningful spell to
foretell the future, & then a doubling
sequence is like, "the power of the generalized
breath, maybe it is." Like if I breathe, I hope …
I hope my inexorable way of living
never becomes the subject
of investigation for
our totalitarian
state.
And now the question (not
worth saving): will
they ever ask me
to donate my
eyebrows?

I Want Something Other Than Time

The jurisdiction
of saying goes against
us. We imagine
in the void of what we want
an end to being. At the same time,
we kept everything.
Soon there would open a narrow body,
unwhole & uncombinable.
It could stop unveiling.
But I'm cultivating these moments for later
(like vapid wires / sarcomic ulcer), so please
don't take it personally that I don't yet
understand this.
Anyway, whatever we say yields our own kind
of ghost, is reduced to acoustical matter
retroactively, or will be. I mean
what we thought mattered about what we
said will be swallowed by the acoustic
revolution to come for a use we can't yet
fathom. But maybe this is all to say
I'm moved by moving, like to blush
in the tentative tracing of
an unsayable frame.
Long-time-ago
puzzle dominating
completion.

I Want Something Other Than Time

Think of a thread
finer by one degree than
what constitutes thread:
it doesn't hold the line, it's not
within our intention.
In what it isn't is a rearrangeability thru
which it proceeds as it begins, increasing
the interim of a lost union, & then
just a moment ago, we are repeating an impression,
we've had a similar feeling & we have to repeat it.
I tried to write an essay that would proceed by this
insight to describe it, but what emerged
was a way of banishing what I could see
such that the force of its expulsion
would resound in its place as though
a matter of principle.
Here though,
in this poem,
my insatiable proximity to these
impassable distances from me itself
feels curbed,
so why do I feel as disturbed as
comforted by this?
Now I'm cupping my book b/c
its rays of quotable pith, b/c
it's another perfect prism
for the reappearance.

I Want Something Other Than Time

Do I feel scolded by
the rain? Fuck no!
Do I feel scolded by tornado
sirens as oversized hail forms
the divots it lands in? Today I do.
I went to the bank today & asked to see
the vaults.
In the teller's plexiglass a reflection caught my
eye & confirmed my purpose.
(I was wanting a dialogue with a can of
sparkling water in plain view of an open
bank vault.)
What I found is that our world is inadequately
on their terms b/c our failing attempts
root almost everything as them.
They, who can never cure us of our torments,
permit me now to trace characters on a
formerly blank piece of paper.
Fort Dietrich in the air of itself, I write.
The existent in the existing, I write,
resists despair by tying itself to its own
forgettable scenery.
It writes us up
(for what
we do
not know).

I Want Something Other Than Time

It's not easy to
translate w/o excess
that direct exposure
to our own body,
a sepulchre full with rapid
articulations, each consisting
of an attachment to pain.
And this is to say that,
as we dissect an eye to define the
anatomy of vision, we
do define suffering by suffering.
I do not work. I do not
eat. Instead,
I wait in the symbolic deciphering
of embodiment as if there is
no body here.
And then, in a sense-knowledge whose
value falls when articulated,
I find I'm planning for an event,
donning ideals, suppressing the distances
within me, covering our bodies
with signs, compunctions,
backing myself
up to
mime in.

I Want Something Other Than Time

From the body cave
to the body boundaries,
we are immersed in the
circumstance of holding our
selves in place.
Let's say we are any three things (replace
as needed), like discourse / velocity / tomb,
repeatedly translated as:
outside / intake / indistinguishing,
& that our cultural context determines
that at any given moment only
two of these three points can be felt.
Under these circumstances how could anyone
continue to be immersed in the effort
of meaning?
And our use of literature as
being in oneself as another that is oneself
constructs an escape from
the pressure put on meaning by
this debt which, calibrated by literature,
wishes instead there were
another word for
light, &
sure, there
is.

I Want Something Other Than Time

I get up feeling
numb, but not really
numb, more like I get up
feeling contempt for a
numbness I'm feeling to produce
this contempt.
This is all felt in a murmur of silence,
a conspicuous denial of substance, an audibly
unspoken refusal to engage.
There was a time in my life, I feel, when I
could've turned this around in a single day,
but now I feel my whole remaining life
won't suffice.
Bataille wrote something like, "I want
to stir the most significant mistrust
against myself," & maybe I'm like that
too, swatting flies against my own face &
head b/c that's where I most notice
them landing.
To not know ourselves,
to hold the appearance of limits
away from ourselves,
is this the way we're
permitted
to continue?

I Want Something Other Than Time

Flux, drained thru
the base of a loss
to fall out again as
this interior.
It goes mind, mind, bug,
& then a final word beyond
its limits & we're done.
A resistance I feel in the automatically
replenishing form, image of us
leaving the room not as the choice
that leaving will have been, but
as the inevitability it is.
And
arriving along the disintegrative
pathos of my thought
like a pleurisy in its letters
is a desire for reciprocity both
met & undone,
is a move where excess feeling
counts itself to open another
fold of freakout, a move
we're too upset to reveal
while it reinsures the pattern.
We've just begun the years counting
down not up.
I should've written this whole thing
in reverse,
against the fabric
its interruptions
fray.

I Want Something Other Than Time

When Michel Serres
points out that disorder
only necessarily destroys
order from order's perspective,
I can feel something other than
my ideas of time experienced
traveling beyond the compass's axis
interrupted.
And in this disruption I hear us telling us
we shouldn't write about it.
About how, for instance, if neither time nor
eternity can let us feel unbound, then perhaps
the whole thing's a question beyond direction,
power, knowledge, pizza,
& how, for instance, if I feel like our gestures
& utterances, chopped & parceled from our
bodies & our bodies' prosthetics, are as
much a political party donation as a
possibility of being, then,
as the passerby pauses to repeat to us,
there is no meaningful then
b/w my no wings to be considered
& my bewildered flight.

I Want Something Other Than Time

I'm like building
a model of my ghost,
like the relation is to
my ghost, not the world I'm
building it in.
I repeat, I can't put myself, or us,
or the world this is in
in my ghost's place.
My ghost doesn't care if I remain an ego,
am I making myself clear?
Everything is already form except for my ghost
who's nothing to me perceptually but a glimpse
of some grimaces covering the formlessness
like some kind of mouth-void.
The inhibitions & the lifting of inhibitions
around what I can say
put & return my parasitical ghost into
each event that happens to or as me.
There's a condition of failure to
all of this: I'm allowed to possess nothing.
In my next incarnation
I want to be ghost instead,
to be schema at the expense of content,
I'll balance a beam
with middle my
mouth.

I Want Something Other Than Time

Not later, I find my
self asking myself,
how do we resist recognizing
only our self in the experience
of our emotions?
Please don't touch me, I whisper,
apple crumble crumbs scattered around me to
retrace my steps.
I destroy everything but the wish for no more
interiority. Meanwhile, an interior sign predicts itself &
comes to pass, & beyond that
something like the analysis of a glacier's regression
threads its measurement slowly thru the entry of what.
And I'm hoping this isn't just fragile, isn't just a
phrase into the verge of vanishing, or
interior to sit by interior as
this is just a place I mostly wouldn't
want to live rolls by.
No, we tell our self, it shadows our suffering
under a cataclysm to come,
an impassable burst of striking thru not
yet struck.
And I'm against myself, as though our confusions
could make our deaths happy, to find myself
saying instead of don't touch me,
I elate in the mystery
of my
disappearance.

I Want Something Other Than Time

Mirror on the
ground, eyes for
sight, I turn both
in the process of vanishing
& they turn too.
Their rhythm goes:
"we live in a dome exchanged w/others."
WTF, other domes or other selves?
Sewers, Abatha, sewers, said Abatha.
A thinning thing is fevering the thought,
a frameless sensitivity running parallel to time,
shifting for balance back & forth
b/w a trauma no longer in service to itself
& a not-wise timelessness drifting
in rotations around it.
Is this a poem about how experience,
bound as it is to projective surfaces,
necessitates & negates a fiction of consciousness?
And I acquaint this question to an
unaskable mystery I feel when
very close to my love's face
I look into my love's face.
Mirror for groundless sight.
How we can't
recover
having met.

I Want Something Other Than Time

Sometimes I dream
of being swallowed up
by a collective & want to
ask, was this our collective dream,
to be held away from our insufficiencies
until at last we sense our bodies' self
as fluid within a system of fluids in
service to itself?
I'm not going to fight my way into this.
Not now, not when alone I feel a secret that,
b/c it can't be fully extorted,
updates itself with trivial constancy.
No, not like this,
when even breaking into heaven
feels degraded as gone.
I'm thrown back again into a bookstore
that's never existed, I think, except for
in the eye of my dreams.
And I can recognize the poetry section,
can lead our voice perfectly towards it.
Browsing there, I'm not thinking the
possible meanings of the books as needed futures,
or wanting to pose their many endings as
some sort of endlessness.
There are millions of us arriving into
quarantine,
& we're all &
each alert
& alive.

I Want Something Other Than Time

It's an incessant
relating to the city
we live in that makes
it feel so irreplaceable.
And us, aren't we a content
making it up, at once
its background & luminous soul?
We watch conspiracies fester in people
to achieve their purpose. My body wasted
in a fit of unfitness, the task goes on w/o me.
Midtown now & I'm painting my cousin,
the famous mime, right before her big show.
It's true.
And in light of the very many years apart,
this feels like my true allotment.
Not portraiture per se, but making us up.
The pores of a face can be
infinitely or can never be totally
glossed.
We make a practice, determined
to avenge our failures, something like
a joke, works right
up until it bursts b/w the two,
& feeling the ground
unsafe, we adjust
to a term of
its
autonomy.

I Want Something Other Than Time

To the extent
the past we were
once of or in
was equally total, partial,
actual, or illusory as
this is now, I'm staying up
really late waiting for this.
I'm simulating an unresounding
room to write unknuckled in
for a loose screenshot of some
beyond the antithesis
order or principle, all
in the broken reference (I
won't call it hope) that I
might pass thru some circle or
mask of the question of experience
& finally, as Merle Hoyleman writes,
"avenge their lottery."
But in this formula, in its move to secure a base,
I think I've flooded the quieter, outer
tunnels in a vocab of addiction, & with them
our path to quit suffering like this.
I go thru all the steps that have
separated my knowledge of myself from
its durations &
I find only a renewed instruction
to renounce myself.

I Want Something Other Than Time

We sat by the water's
edge to feel we were
at the city's edge, but
this city's song wasn't much
to be sung, it had no
edge to it, so we sat there quietly,
desiring the day away in a
trivial thoughtlessness.
Sitting there we remember nothing & now
in a pulse we feel is within us, constituting,
we sense a moment later we'll say
we're within it, constellated.
From another time I see us sitting there
on the banks of the water in a mess of
shadows cast by the other banks behind us
where, on our walk to the water, it was
confirmed:
their drivers would bum us a smoke,
the bankers wouldn't.
Plied now by a wide-open screen which
goes way far back, I'm like a gutter
that streams down from a third floor
laundry & all the way posts:
"If I'm always making space for
something to happen, why do I keep
thinking this space
as future?"

I Want Something Other Than Time

What remains to
be seen is a mutating
figure b/c of constant
relation, is figure b/c of
relation, & our relation is
figured here as collision, collusion
b/w our sense of aloneness, our singular
allotment, & our sense of complicity in shared &
appropriative moves
rising at the flow of mind, impossible to only
intend or be beyond intentions.
We aren't types of people joined to,
we're a part
of or to a vibratory hydraulics system &
neither will prevail.
Water draws from its own spray for its
own spray sometimes,
as I lean into the image of an instant
to substitute myself for its duration.
If only we could be pressed, I say,
into the phantasm of each others' cut-outs,
knowing well I'm a willing
phantom for precisely such pressure.
If only the turbulence of a language which
surrounds us within us could be visualized
rolling in it,
with it in its hand,
b/w us.

I Want Something Other Than Time

I'll ask again,
does a situation exist?
A pretensc, we feel,
divides experience
& paralyzes the question.
Experience, we feel, in a waving
interchange, becomes
interchangeable with itself
& is unattainable.
But I don't stop soliciting asparagus for
my mouth just b/c it retains some essence of
itself on the way out.
I mean, a moment doesn't arrive, it
overtakes itself as another, right?
It shatters the encumbrance of
having passed by carrying something not
itself from an nother now.
In this way we appear as news to
ourself, yet feel we represent our own
dismissal.
So no, I'll no longer ring the bell of
presence as healing fit for an
irritable cartilage I've got in mind.
This body & vine detach say,
pushed to insulate
a sanctimonious
gone.

I Want Something Other Than Time

This is precise.
No sequence that
doesn't sentence itself,
no point to itself along the
sequence of its duration.
When I first began writing
this dimension would overcome me
like a mask.
I seemed to be an endless fabric
ripped into the thing &
perhaps, I thought, one day I could
submit my whole self to it in
an accident.
But what exists is already kind of closed up.
The order I made was borne by the spirit
to be delivered in two days.
It was for something private, this order.
Something private & molting.
The voice said, "like a mask,"
a limit to its own.
No solitude in which one
could proceed
from.

I Want Something Other Than Time

I'm keeping one
eye on the unknowable
readings of this text,
& what confusion has kept me
here this past year, opaque as
perpetuity, has kept my eyes from
some other tune than this.
To write this is only a way
of knowing the clearing is a part
of knowing nothing, but it's also like saying
my tumor is prophetic, &
shifting the screen from one aerial shot
of the ocean to another, it's
the move that's matter.
If I were to characterize this as I write
this text that's almost gone, almost ready to remain,
I might say a pseudonym surrounds the page,
tells me defend the face head-on with song.
But a pseudonym can't ever really relax into its
eternal squalor. It holds a cushion, hidden
in the president's never-used cello, for
ransom, & never knows which.
A conflict in this order with the order to arrive.
It locates a point where
my fixation on the unknowable becomes a
social violence, unpardonable.
It's precisely the point where
all I've learned to do is disengage.
Page already knows
we know this
is the end.

Acknowledgments

This book began being written in February of 2017 in Stillwater, Oklahoma, and was repeatedly rewritten thru March of 2018. It remained primarily a handwritten manuscript until September of 2018 when, in Kenosha, Wisconsin, at the request of Peter Gizzi (to whom I'm especially grateful), I typed it up. A quite expansive explanation of the process of composition accompanies the special handwritten edition of the book. Versions of some of these poems have appeared in *Marsh Hawk Review*, *The Continental Review*, *Alienocene*, and *Paradise Now*.

I have since about the age of ten experienced myself as a person constituted b/w & entirely by others, and so it is still that w/o the many many friends who have kindly read, listened to, commented on, &/or encouraged the poems that constitute this book, neither it nor this I making some claim to it would exist. As such I am grateful to the following many many who interacted variously with these poems as they were being made (& to others I must've mistakenly not recalled while going thru email & memory this afternoon, please forgive me): Joshua Beckman, Steve Benson Anselm Berrigan, Stacy Blint, Timothy Bradford, David Brazil, Brandon Brown, Bryon Cherry, CAConrad, Corina Copp, Julia Dauer, Thom Donovan, Ian Dreiblatt, Jordan Dunn, Thomas Fink, Lisa Fishman, Jonathan Gaboury, Renee Gladman, Tirzah Goldenberg, Andy Gricevich, Kate Hallemeier, Roberto Harrison, Mike Hauser, Hailey Higdon, Crag Hill, Andrew Hladky, Grant Jenkins, Bethany Kanter, Stacy Kidd, Nathan Knapp, Francis Landy, Hank Lazer, Gabriel Levin, Ben McGuire, Rick Meier, Holly Melgard, Jeff Menne, Frédéric Neyrat, Nathaniel Otting, Julie Patton,

Zack Piper, Tim Ramick, Ariel Resnikoff, Ariel Ross, Judah Rubin, Lauren Russell, Robert Sniderman, Wayne Stables, Jordan Stempleman, Alexandra Tatarsky, Vanessa Thill, Steve Timm, Anna Vitale, Cathy Wagner, Dana Ward, Karen Weiser, Matvei Yankelevich, & Joey Yearous-Algozin. A deep thank you to everyone at Ugly Duckling Presse for their labor & for the communities of texts and persons they construct & inhabit which I feel honored to take some part in. An extra thanks to Daniel Owen and Sarah Lawson whose caring conversation & editorial guidance around this book is invaluable to me. And finally a thanks beyond thanks to Lisa Hollenbach whose contribution to this book is so multidimensional, intertwined in language & feeling as we are, that it feels to me beyond measure.

ON ...
NOWABLE, & W...
HIS TEXT, & KE...
FUSION HAS KEP...
PAST YEAR, OPAQUE ...
PETUITY, HAS KEPT MY E...
E OTHER TUNE THAN THIS.
WRITE THIS IS ONLY A WAY OF KNOWIN...
CLEARING IS A PART OF KNOWING MY...
HING, BUT IT'S ALSO LIKE SAYING MY...
PROPHETIC, & SHIFTING THE SCREEN FROM ...
RIAL SHOT OF THE OCEAN TO ANOTHER, IT'...
MOVE THAT'S MATTER.
I WERE TO CHARACTERIZE THIS AS I WR...
T'S ALMOST GONE, ALMOST READY TO ...
MIGHT SAY A PSEUDONYM SURROUN...
LS ME DEFEND THE FACE HEAD-ON ...
A PSEUDONYM CAN'T EVER REALLY R...
RNAL SQUALOR. IT HOLDS A CUSHIO...
THE PRESIDENT'S NEVER-USED CELL...
NSOM, & NEVER KNOWS WHICH...
ONFLICT IN THIS ORDER WITH THE ...
ARRIVE. IT LOCATES A POINT WHE...
ATION ON THE UNKNOWABLE BEC...
CIAL VIOLENCE, UNPARDONABLE.
S PRECISELY THE POINT WHERE A...
ARNED TO DO IS DISENGAGE.
PAGE ALREADY KN...
KNOW